010

The Rainy day Book

Jane Bull

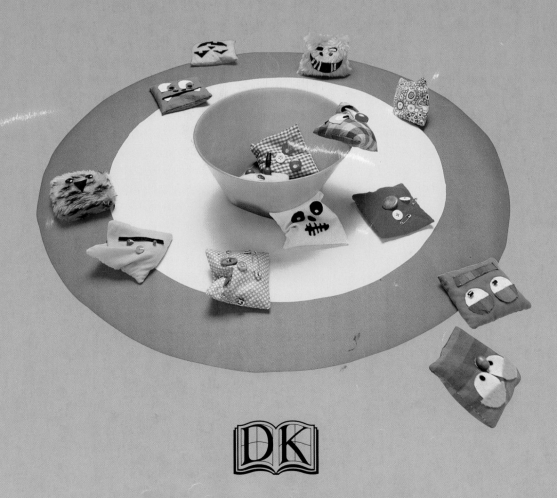

DK

A Dorling Kindersley Book

LONDON, NEW YORK, MUNICH,
MELBOURNE, AND DELHI

DESIGN • Jane Bull
EDITOR • Penelope Arlon
PHOTOGRAPHY • Andy Crawford
DESIGN ASSISTANCE • Sadie Thomas

PUBLISHING MANAGER • Sue Leonard
MANAGING ART EDITOR • Clare Sheddon
PRODUCTION • Shivani Pandey
DTP DESIGNER • Almudena Díaz

For Charlotte, Billy, and James

First published in Great Britain in 2003 by
Dorling Kindersley Limited
80 Strand,
London WC2R 0RL

A Penguin Company

2 4 6 8 10 9 7 5 3 1

A CIP catalogue record for this book
is available from the British Library

ISBN: 0-7513-6840-7

Colour reproduction by GRB Editrice S.r.l., Verona, Italy
Printed and bound in Italy by L.E.G.O.

See our complete
catalogue at
www.dk.com

OK!
load it up

prepare to keep out the
rainy day gloom

Bright ideas for a rainy day...

weave away the gloom...

...and pour out some fun

Rainy day survival kit

Be prepared - Collect bits and pieces regularly, such as all these things around the page, so that when it rains, you have lots to work with.

Look for Bob on this page
Find out who he is on page 44

Materials and tools used in the book

Felt pens • Plain paper • Face paints and sponges
• Paint brushes • Wallpaper paste • Glue
• Scraps of material • Knitting and sewing needles
• Scissors • String • Wool • All kinds of paper
• Buttons and beads • Materials to cook with

4

How to survive a
Rainy Day

The rain is pouring down and there's simply nowhere to go. What are you going to do? You could watch television OR you could have some fun.

Why not feast on cookies, take a dot for a walk, say "hello" to your hands, get wrapped up in string, and if it's still raining after all that, you can try catching it!

Rainy day doodles

You won't believe what you can do with a doodle! Just put the pen down on the page and wave and wriggle away. Let your pen run free!

Take a dot for a walk

and colour in the spaces

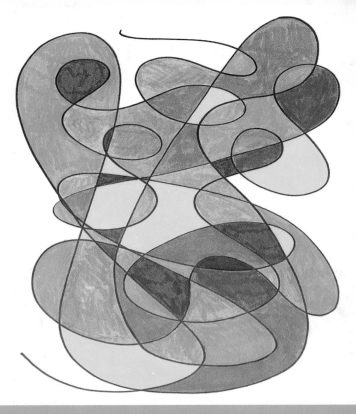

Lines and loops
t may look complicated but that's the beauty of it. It's easy!
Draw straight lines across the paper, then draw a loopy
shape over the top. Now colour in alternate shapes.

Take a dot for another walk
Put your pen down and let your hand move freely across
a page. Feel free to cross lines and cut up circles. Now
colour in each shape and watch the pattern come to life.

Eye-boggling spiral
Draw lots of circles from the centre, each getting bigger,
then draw lines outwards, like a web. Colour them in.

weaving waves
Draw wavy lines across the page and down. Then
colour in alternate squares for bulging patterns.

Hello hands!

Face paints

Forget your face, paint your hands instead! Turn your fingers into little personalities.

Water for thinning paint.

Fine and thick brush and a washa felt pen.

Sponges to paint large areas.

wet the sponge, and dab it in the paint.

Paint your hand all over with the sponge.

Add the details with a paint bru

Football crazy

Lets go!

My ball

Yes!

I liked the sliding tackle. Good game Jim!

Hints and tips

• Choose a good quality face paint.
• Look at your hands and decide on a shape that suits your fingers.
• Use a damp sponge to cover large areas. Wait for it to dry before you paint the details.
• Use a washable felt pen for outlines and faces.
• Clean the paints off with soap and water.

Pretty Polly

Creatures with beaks and long necks work well too, like this parrot. Try other birds – a cockerel or a pink flamingo.

Elephant fingers

I am an alien

paper pots

There's paper all around you. Don't throw it away, recycle it!

Sweet wrappers

Coloured foil

Envelopes

Coloured paper

Comics

Magazines

Newspaper

How to make a pot

Vaseline

1. Blow up a balloon, spread vaseline over it, brush over some paste, and half cover it with paper.

See page 46 for more about paste.

Wallpaper paste

2. Cover the balloon with about six layers. Leave it to dry in a warm place.

3. Take the balloon out and trim off the rough edges.

4. Make a base with a strip of card, tape it on, and cover it with paste and paper.

5. Cut card for ears, tape in place, and again cover with paste and paper.

Decorate inside and out.

Box rooms

where your toys can live. Decorate and furnish them with bits and bobs

Find a cardboard box

Measure up the paper

Use wrapping paper or paint your own wallpaper.

Draw and cut out windows

⭐ **Ask an Adult** to help cut the thick card.

you will need

For the house itself:
- A cardboard box
- Scissors, ruler, and pen
- Decorated wallpaper
- Material for the carpet
- Glue

Decorate the walls

Glue the wallpaper to the inside of the box.

Cover the floor

Cut a window in the box.

A face flannel makes a very good carpet.

Ahh, home sweet home

Come in out of the rain

All I need now is a comfy chair

How to make scrap furniture

Collect boxes, cartons, and other bits and pieces that are going to be thrown away – imagine how many you will gather over the weeks for those rainy days. You'll have a great collection.

Small boxes

Create a cupboard from a small box. Cut out a door and attach a split pin handle onto it.

Lamp

Stick a straw in a cotton reel and pop a paper cake case on top.

Armchair

Paint four matchboxes and glue them together.

Table

Stick a large lid onto a drinks bottle lid with a piece of modelling clay.

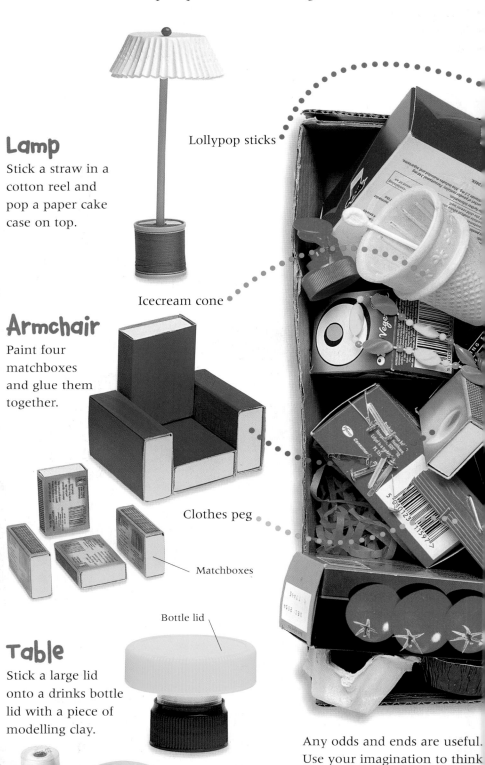

Lollypop sticks

Icecream cone

Clothes peg

Matchboxes

Bottle lid

Modelling clay

Any odds and ends are useful. Use your imagination to think of other bits of furniture that can go inside your box room.

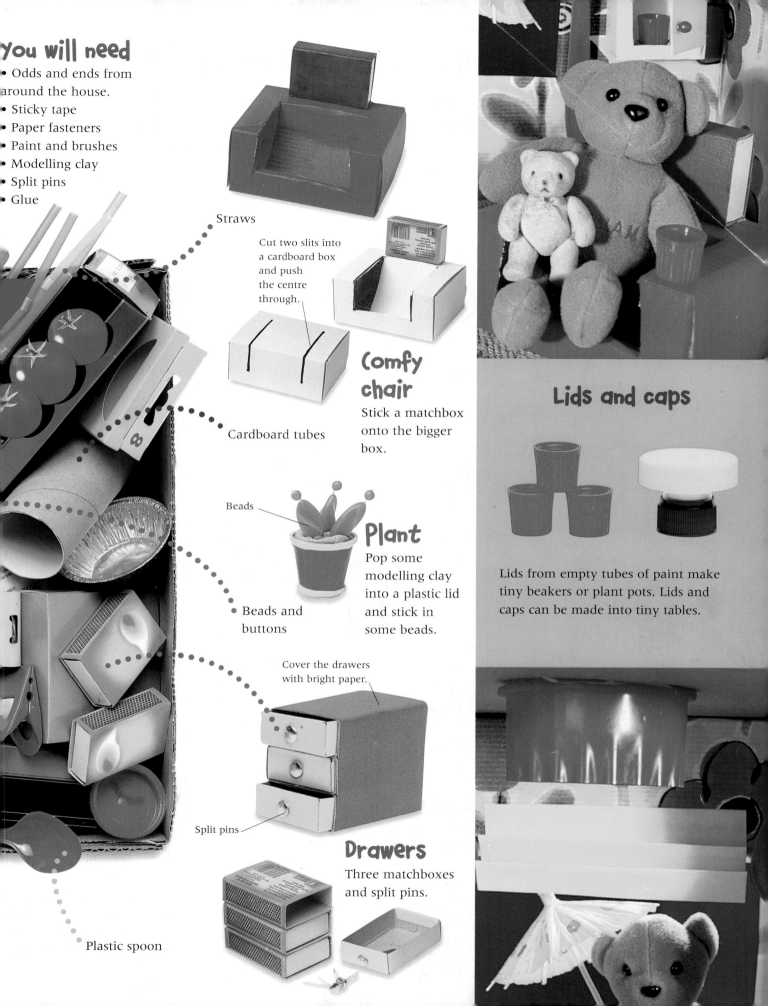

you will need

- Odds and ends from around the house.
- Sticky tape
- Paper fasteners
- Paint and brushes
- Modelling clay
- Split pins
- Glue

Straws

Cut two slits into a cardboard box and push the centre through.

Cardboard tubes

Comfy chair

Stick a matchbox onto the bigger box.

Beads

Plant

Pop some modelling clay into a plastic lid and stick in some beads.

Beads and buttons

Cover the drawers with bright paper.

Split pins

Drawers

Three matchboxes and split pins.

Plastic spoon

Lids and caps

Lids from empty tubes of paint make tiny beakers or plant pots. Lids and caps can be made into tiny tables.

Pets corner

Create cages for your furry toys
– open your very own animal hospital.

You will need
- Cardboard box
- Glue, tape
- Scissors
- Split pins
- Black pen

Cosy hutch

Help your cuddly pets feel right at home by cutting strips of scrap paper for their bed. Give them bowls for food and water and every so often let them out for a cuddle. The good thing about toy pets is that they never need cleaning out!

Draw swirls on the cardboard with a black pen to make it look like wood.

Cage door

Make a cage door for your hutch with strips of card. Measure your box and cut two long pieces of card and two shorter pieces.

The long pieces must be about 6 cm (2 in) longer than the length of the box.

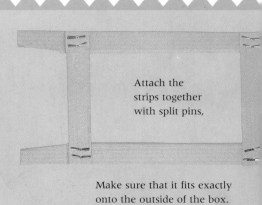

Attach the strips together with split pins,

Make sure that it fits exactly onto the outside of the box.

It's feeding time!

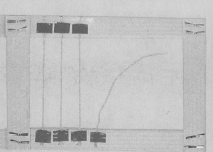

Use wool as your caged bars by sticking
lengths to the top and bottom of the back.

Attach the cage
door by gluing the
flaps to the side of the
box. Alternatively you
could use split pins.

Make a latch
out of card
and a split
pin.

17

Salt dough

Four activities in one

1. Mixing
2. Modelling
3. Cooking
4. Painting

Mix the dough and squeeze it into any shape you like. Hours of doughy fun.

To make the dough you will need

water
200 ml
(1/3 pint)

Salt
300 g (10 oz)

Flour
300 g
(10 oz)

Oil
2 tsp

Put all of th
ingredients
into a bowl

Squeeze the
mixture
together.

Pat it int
a ball.

Roll it out

Now have a play!

Make a good **impression**

Play with your dough

Roll it, rake it,
squash it, squeeze it.
Look around your house
for objects to press into
the dough. You can
create all sorts of effects
and shapes and if you
don't like them, roll it up
and start again.

If the dough
gets sticky, sprinkle
on some flour.

Bear necessities

Make the bear shapes.

Squash a paperclip onto the back.

Stick them together.

Bake the bear then paint it.

Tie on some string.

Baking your shapes

Place your shapes on a baking tray.

If the shapes are big they will take longer to cook, and if they are delicate they may break more easily, so keep them small and chunky.

Let them cool down before you paint them.

☆ **Ask an Adult** to help with the oven.

Bake for 20 minutes (180°C/350°F/Gas mark 4)

Painting and decorating

When the baked dough has cooled down, you can paint it with poster or acrylic paint. Try mixing a little PVA glue with the paint (about 1 part PVA to 2 parts paint), this will make it tough and shiny.

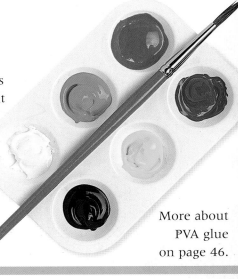

More about PVA glue on page 46.

Keeping your dough

Save it for a rainy day

You can save your unbaked dough by covering it in plastic wrap. It will keep for about two weeks.

21

Sweet dough

Dough you can eat - make these tasty shortbread biscuits.

Flour

Yum Yum

Roll the dough into a ball and squash it flat.

Squash with a fork

Biscuit Mix

Makes 12-16
Plain biscuits
300 g (6 oz) plain flour
200 g (4 oz) butter
100 g (2 oz) sugar

Put the flour, sugar, and butter into a bowl.
Squeeze them together with your fingers until they come together to make a ball of dough.
Shape your biscuits and decorate them.
Place them on a baking tray.
Cook for 15 minutes (160°C/325°F/Gas mark 3)
Cool them on a cooling rack and TUCK IN!

Butter

For chocolate biscuits:
250 g (5 oz) plain flour
50 g (2 oz) cocoa powder
100 g (4 oz) butter
50 g (2 oz) sugar

For coconut biscuits:
Add 50 g (2 oz) coconut to to mix.

Sugar

 Ask an Adult to help with the oven.

Leave some space between your biscuits.

22

Making patterns

Try sugar strands and colourful sweets for decoration, or use plain and chocolate dough together to create spots and stripes.

Sugar strands

Choc drops

Coconut

Choc sweets

Big chocolate sweets

23

use the furniture

It will give extra height to the chutes.

Grr

24

all set for the Domino Run? Go!

A spectacular run

Push the car at the top of the stool and watch it go! Set up the dominoes so that as one falls, it will knock down the next and so on. The aim is to create a set that will fall from beginning to end without stopping.

You will need

- Dominoes
- Boxes
- Cardboard tubes
- Building bricks
- Bits and pieces to help the run.

what will happen?
Turn to page 43

Get weaving

wonderful webs in rainbow colours.

Paper plate

wool

A paper plate and scraps of wool create a rainbow web to brighten up your day.

To weave a web
you will need
- A paper plate or a circle of c
- Scraps of wool
- Darning needle

26

1

Draw out a zig-zag edge around the plate and cut out the triangles.

2

See page 46 for other ways to start off.

knot

Loop the wool around two opposite spikes, making sure they cross in the middle and tie a kot in the centre.

3

Keep crossing the wool from spike to spike, making sure the wool crosses through the middle.

The wool will go around this one next.

4

Keep going backwards and forwards across the plate.

5

Turn your plate over and it should look like this. Tie the end of the wool into a knot.

6

Thread a piece of wool onto a needle. From the middle, weave the needle between the strands.

It will look odd at first but after about six rows, it will even out.

7

As you weave, make sure you pull it tight into the middle

8

Knot a new piece of wool to the last one and just keep on weaving.

use up your old scraps

Continue weaving different colours until there's no more room.

keep on weaving

Looms are frames used for weaving fabric. Make a simple loom and have a go at creating a piece of fabric and then start to weave anything you can find!

Home-made loom

A shoebox lid is ideal. Cut the same number of slits on opposite ends then thread wool backwards and forwards.

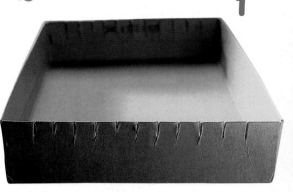

1

 Ask an Adult to cut the slits, they may need to use a sharp knife.

2

Wrap the wool around the first slit to hold it in place.

3

Keep going up and down.

4

Thread the wool above and below the main strands and forward and back.

Now try weaving other things that you can find.

6

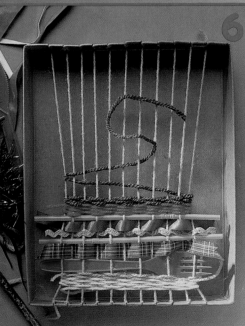

Weave and weave until you reach the top.

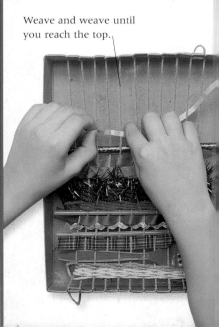

A work of weaving art — attach it to the wall for all to see.

Ribbon

Wool

Plastic Knife

Pencil

Tinsel

Straw

Fancy Ribbon

Plastic Fork

Scrap bags

These floppy bag people
are made from scraps of
left-over material and filled
with dried beans.

"Try me I'm
very filling",
yell the lentils.

30

Play with us,
we're full of beans!

Throw together a scrap bag

Here, catch!

To make a bag

Use the scrap bag pattern to measure the size of your bag. Cut out a piece of fabric and fold it in half.

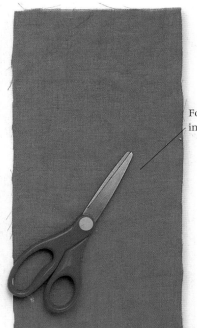

Fold it in half.

LEAVE A HOLE

STITCHING LINE

Scrap bag pattern
Follow this
pattern to help
you with the size.

FOLD THE FABRIC HERE

STITCHING LINE

LEAVE A HOLE

Leave an opening at the top.

Back stitch around the open sides.

Turn the bag inside out.

Fill it up with lentil beans.

To finish it off, stitch up the hole at the top.

Pin it together

Sew up the sides

Turn inside out and fill up

Close it up

Back stitch

A good stitch to use is back stitch because it completely seals the sides. Don't be fooled into thinking you can do a simple running stitch, if you do the beans will fall out!

See page 46 for back stitch instructions.

Sew or use PVA glue to attach the faces.

Scrap bag games

Target practice

Set up a target area around a bucket and challenge your family to score high. Make up the rules yourself!

Juggling

Start with two then build up your bags. A perfect practice for a rainy day.

Play catch

Throw a bag for a friend to catch. If they miss they go down on one knee, miss again they go down on two knees, and so on until they are lying down.

Bad luck! To score 100 it must go right into the bowl.

100

50

25

Good shot, that's 100 points!

33

String things

what a wind up! See-through string balls and fluffy pom-poms, there's a whole new woolly world to discover.

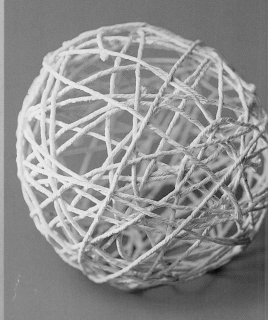

Juggle those pom-poms!

How to make a string thing

You will need • Balloon • String or wool • Wallpaper paste • Vaseline

Blow up a balloon and spread Vaseline all over it – this will stop the string sticking to the balloon.

Mix up a bowl of wallpaper paste.

Cut some lengths of string, about 60 cm (22 in) long.

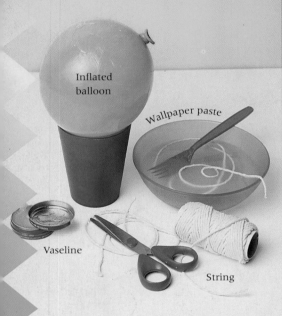

Inflated balloon

Wallpaper paste

Vaseline

String

Dip the string into the paste, then wrap it around the balloon.

Watch out!
This bit gets messy

Add More and more and more string until you have enough.

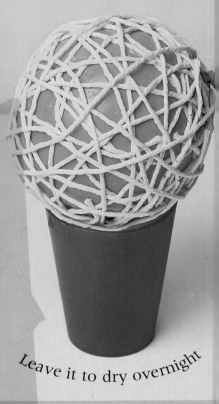

Leave it to dry overnight

How to make a Pom-pom

You will need • Thin card • Wool

Tip: The larger the discs, the bigger your pom-pom will turn out.

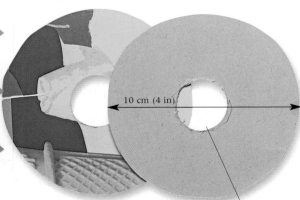

10 cm (4 in)

Knot the wool in place.

Add more wool unt complet cove

Cut two discs from thin card.

Cut a 3 cm (1 1/5 in) diameter hole in the middle.

Put the two discs of card together.

Wind the wool around and around – through the middle and over the top.

When the string is dry...

pop the balloon!

Put the scissors between the two discs.

Tip For multi-colours add different wool as you wind.

Snip away any long bits.

Snip the wool all the way around.

Hold it firmly in the middle.

Open up the discs slightly.

Tie a piece of wool tightly around the middle.

Pull the card off and fluff up the wool.

A pom-pom – it's magic!

why not make a friendship bracelet for your favourite friend?

Knitting

Master the skill of knitting. Begin with your fingers and thumbs and work up to needles. As well as wool, you will need lots of patience, so DON'T give up.

Finger knitting

This is also called finger crochet. Wind the wool around your thumb twice then pick up the first loop and take it over the second. Keep repeating this until it has grown to the length you want.

1 Wind the wool around your thumb twice.

2 Pick up the first loop.

3 Take it over the second loop.

4 Keep going.

5 Carefully pull the wool.

6 Pull the wool so the stitch is secure on your finger.

7 Repeat the steps. The first loop is there, so wind the wool to make the second.

Use two pieces of different coloured wool to make a multicoloured wristband.

It's growing

As you repeat the steps, the bracelet will grow and grow.

Knit a blanket

Once you have got the hang of finger knitting, you will have a good idea how to cast on to needles and start knitting. Using plain stitch you can make a finger puppet from a single square, and if you get really ambitious you can make lots of squares to make a blanket.

I'm in stitches!

How to knit

Follow these knitting instructions and you'll be using plain stitch with standard needles. Once you have got the hang of it there will be no stopping you – you'll be well and truly hooked!

You will need

- Knitting needles size 4 mm (no.9)
- Ball of wool

Casting on – this is how you get the stitches onto the needle.

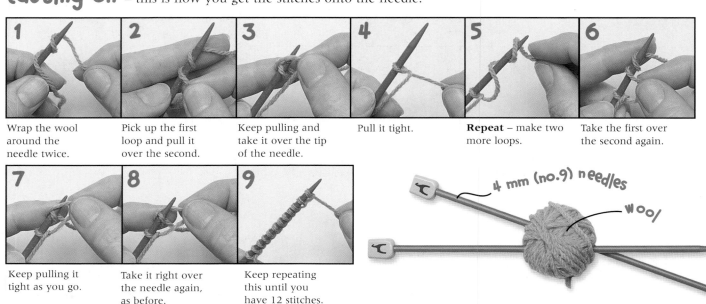

1 Wrap the wool around the needle twice.

2 Pick up the first loop and pull it over the second.

3 Keep pulling and take it over the tip of the needle.

4 Pull it tight.

5 **Repeat** – make two more loops.

6 Take the first over the second again.

7 Keep pulling it tight as you go.

8 Take it right over the needle again, as before.

9 Keep repeating this until you have 12 stitches.

4 mm (no.9) needles

wool

Plain stitch

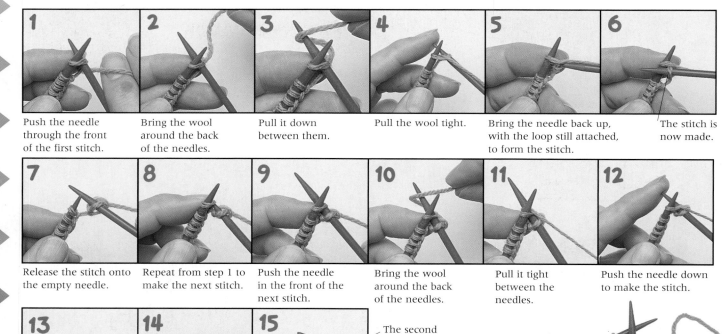

1 Push the needle through the front of the first stitch.

2 Bring the wool around the back of the needles.

3 Pull it down between them.

4 Pull the wool tight.

5 Bring the needle back up, with the loop still attached, to form the stitch.

6 The stitch is now made.

7 Release the stitch onto the empty needle.

8 Repeat from step 1 to make the next stitch.

9 Push the needle in the front of the next stitch.

10 Bring the wool around the back of the needles.

11 Pull it tight between the needles.

12 Push the needle down to make the stitch.

13 Bring the needle back and to the front again.

14 You now have two stitches.

15 Keep doing this until you finish the row.

The second stitch is now made.

Keep Going!

Repeat these steps until you reach the length you want.

Casting off – do this when you have reached the length you want.

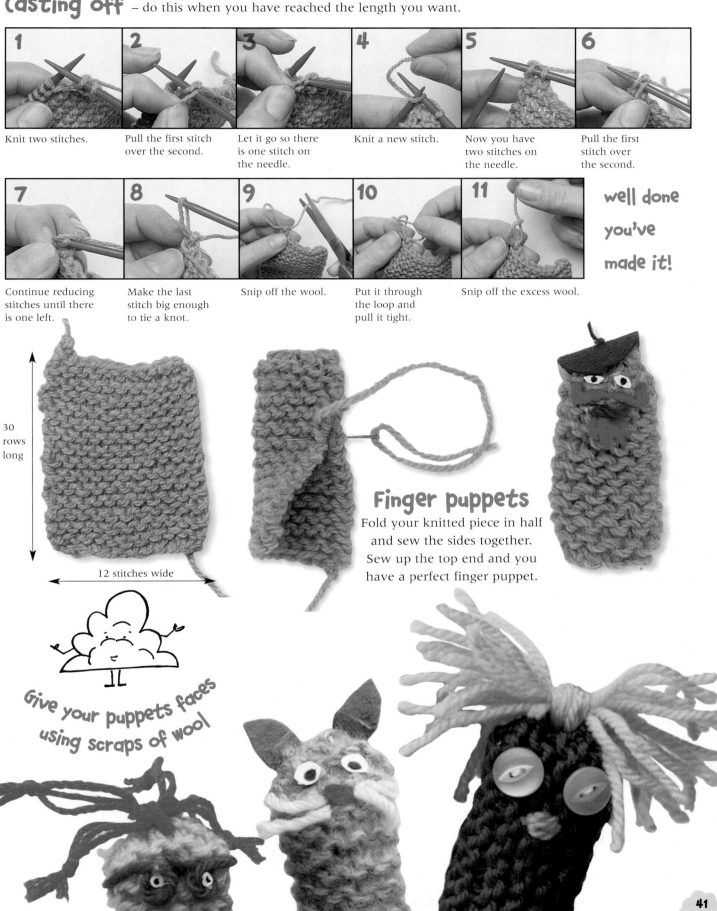

1 Knit two stitches.

2 Pull the first stitch over the second.

3 Let it go so there is one stitch on the needle.

4 Knit a new stitch.

5 Now you have two stitches on the needle.

6 Pull the first stitch over the second.

7 Continue reducing stitches until there is one left.

8 Make the last stitch big enough to tie a knot.

9 Snip off the wool.

10 Put it through the loop and pull it tight.

11 Snip off the excess wool.

well done you've made it!

30 rows long

12 stitches wide

Finger puppets

Fold your knitted piece in half and sew the sides together. Sew up the top end and you have a perfect finger puppet.

Give your puppets faces using scraps of wool

41

Tunnels and ramps can be made from cardboard tubes, either cut in half or whole.

The Domino effect

Now it's time to see what happens when you knock the first little car down the ramp. Watch out!

Domino tip

Be very, very careful when you lay the dominoes out. If you make a mistake, you may have to start again.

It's a complete mess!

It doesn't stop!

Away it goes!

The car hits the dominoes, the dominoes ram the car, and whoosh! It flies through the tunnel, straight into the people standing at the bottom!

Down the tube

Roar....yum yum!

Chain reaction

Everything is all over the place, as one goes the others follow. What a mess and what a noise!

Crash and its over!

The grand finale

The dominoes crash into the truck, which rolls down the ramp, knocks into the tube carrying the strainer full of sweets, which falls and the dinosaur gets his meal. Phew!

Activity centres – jars packed full of fun

Jars are perfect for filling with lots of little things for your craft projects. Alternatively, fill one up with games, such as dice and cards – useful for those rainy days.

Cards, counters, and quizzes

Beads, buttons, and ribbons

where's Bob?

A game of hide and seek
If you look carefully throughout this book, you will see Bob popping up on certain spreads. Have you seen him yet? The pages he is on are listed on page 48.

Come and get me!

Memory game

Look at these objects for 30 seconds. Now close the book and see how many you can remember. How did you score?

How many can you remember?

Try this on your family. Prepare a tray of objects. Let them study it for 30 seconds. **Time's up!** Quickly cover it with a cloth and the one who can remember all the objects is the winner!

Take a **potato** and make...

Potato heads

Use buttons, cocktail sticks, hairclips, faces from magazines, or anything else you can think of to dress up your potatoes.

Pin the faces in place.

A potato pooch

Potato bake

Scrub and wash a potato. Put it straight in the oven set at 190°C/375°F/Gas mark 5. Bake for about an hour, or until it's soft inside. Take it out and fill it up with cheese.

Cheese and chives on the top.

Don't put on too much paint.

Potato patterns

Cut a potato in half and draw a shape on the inside with felt pen. Carefully cut it out with a knife – remember to cut around your design. Brush paint onto the surface and press it onto some paper.

Keep designs simple

45

All about glue

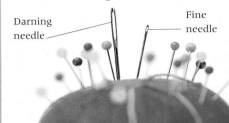

Glue
stick

Wallpaper
paste

All-purpose
glue

wallpaper paste

You can buy this paste in bags from any hardware shop. Put about a tablespoon of the flakes into a bowl and add water until it blends in. It should be thick enough to brush onto a surface.

Glue stick

This is a very clean glue and is best for paper as it won't make it crinkle.

All-purpose glue

This is not only a strong glue, it also smells strong too. Use it for gluing cardboard pieces together.

PVA glue

PVA is very useful glue that works on fabric and card. Mixed with a bit of water it is a good varnish, and mixed with paint, it will give the coloured surface a shiny finish.

Threading a needle

Darning
needle

Fine
needle

This gadget helps you thread a needle, You can get them anywhere that sells cotton.

Push the fine wire through the eye.

Push the needle down to the metal.

Thread your yarn through the wire.

Now just pull the threader and the needle apart and you've done it - easy!

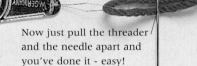

Carry on pulling and then removed the wire threader.

Sewing backstich

Knot
end of
cotton
push t
needle
down
up thr
the fa

Pull th
needle
the wa
throug
the kn

Place
needle
betwe
knot a
the da
cotton

Bring
needle
ahead
dangli
cotton

Repea
steps
sew o
few st
to fini

Get weaving
(page 27)
Quick start and finish
If you have trouble getting your weaving started, use sticky tape to hold the wool in place.

Tape the wool to the back of the plate.

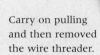
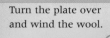

Turn the plate over and wind the wool.

When you have finished turn the plate over.

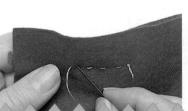

How to make a rain catcher

Take a plastic bottle – one with a flat bottom is the best.

Ask an Adult to help you cut the bottle.

Cut the bottle into two pieces as shown.

Turn the top over and place it back into the bottle base.

Make a dip stick from a wooden spoon. Measure and draw out 1 cm (^{1}/2 in) spaces with a pen.

Pop a drop of food colouring into the bottle so that you can see the water easily.

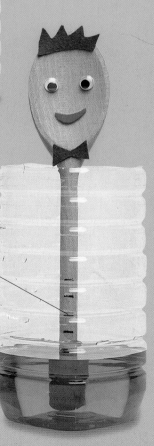

Rain catcher

Rain, rain, go away

If the rain won't go away, make yourself a gauge to measure just how much has fallen. Place some pebbles around the bottom to keep it stable, and check the depth each day against the dip stick.

Index

Did you spot Bob?

Look for him on pages:
4, 17, 24, 39, 42, 44, and 46.

Acknowledgements

With thanks to...
Maisie Armah, Charlotte Bull, Billy Bull
James Bull, Luke Bower, and
Sorcha Lyons for performing the
projects on their rainy days off.

All images © Dorling Kindersley.
For further information see:
www.dkimages.com